A*NTIQUE* *C*ARS

by

illust

HE

Library of Congress Cataloging in Publication Data

Jackson, Robert B.
    Antique cars.

    SUMMARY: Presents a brief history of the automobile
and discusses the features of the early models which
have made them valuable as antiques.
    1. Automobiles — History — Juvenile literature.
[1. Automobiles — History] I. Title.
TL147.J32   629.22′22′09   75-12179
ISBN 0-8098-2105-2

Acknowledgment

The photograph on page 41 is reproduced through the cour-
tesy of General Motors Corporation. Other photographs are by
the author.

Contents

1 / *The Appeal of Antique Automobiles*

THE CARS START TO ASSEMBLE for the show early in the morning. A few of the very oldest arrive in trucks or aboard trailers, but most chug briskly on the field under their own power. There are black carriages on high wooden wheels that look as if they would be better off behind a horse; turn-of-the-century automobiles with upswept rear seats and sparkling brass radiators; splendid open-bodied touring cars of the Twenties and big boxy sedans of the Thirties — two-seaters, limousines, sports cars, station wagons, steamers, electric cars, even old-fashioned fire trucks, one of them complete with a barking Dalmatian dog.

All these fascinating vehicles park in long rows

across the still-wet grass; crowds of spectators begin to collect, and another antique car show is about to get under way. Such outdoor automotive exhibitions are becoming more and more popular in the United States for several reasons.

First of all, most Americans have loved cars since the days of those horseless carriages. And now that at least one motor vehicle exists for every two people in the United States and one of every seven jobs is in some way related to automobiles, more of the population than ever is car-minded.

But this constantly increasing number of automobiles has helped cause high accident rates,

Outdoor antique car shows are becoming increasingly popular in the United States.

traffic snarls and air pollution, not to mention a possible energy shortage. In contrast antique cars date from a happier time when we did not yet realize how serious these problems were going to be; and for this reason many people prefer old cars to current models.

An even more attractive feature of old cars is their individuality. Antique automobiles vary widely in construction, appearance and performance as compared to the standardized vehicles of today, all of which are pretty much alike. Usually designed by one man instead of by committees and computers like modern automobiles, antique cars are generally much more distinctive and have far greater character as a result.

Nearly everyone agrees about this strong appeal of old automobiles. Older spectators like to look at antique cars because they remember driving or riding in them when they were young. Younger viewers are interested to see earlier versions of what has become a central feature of their daily lives; and enthusiasts of all ages admire the skilled craftsmanship shown in the restoration of the cars to their exact original condition.

Some confusion does exist as to just which cars should be called "antique," though. While the public tends to apply the word generally to *all* old automobiles, the organizations of old-car owners are much more specific. The Antique Automobile Club of America, for instance, classifies only those cars built before 1930 as antique. You will see automobiles made between 1930 and 1950 at AACA meets, it is true: but they are officially called either "Production Cars" or "Classic Cars." The classification schemes of the many other old-car groups are apt to vary, and state requirements for "antique" license plates can be still different, thus making the term even more indefinite.

The fourteen antique cars described in the following three chapters were chosen to represent the first forty years of the American automobile, 1893 to 1932. Included are some of the most historically significant manufacturers, models and mechanical advances of that period. A few automobiles and incidents that are not so important appear as well, not only because they are amusing in themselves but also because they illustrate the engaging variety and individualism of nearly all old cars.

2 / *Automotive Pioneers*

Duryea. The automobile was not created at one specific point in history by a single individual but was developed gradually over a period of years by a number of inventors in several countries. After the work of earlier contributors has been recognized, credit for the first practical gasoline automobile is generally awarded to Karl Benz (1885) and Gottlieb Daimler (1886) of Germany.

Identifying the first successful gasoline automobile in the United States is also difficult because many men were tinkering on similar vehicles, all at just about the same time. Still, most historians now give the honor to the Duryea car of 1893 (photo).

Charles E. and J. Frank Duryea were brothers

who had come to Springfield, Massachusetts, because they were in the bicycle business, like so many of the other automotive pioneers. Charles, the elder, was a bicycle manufacturer back in Peoria, Illinois; and young Frank was an expert bicycle mechanic and toolmaker. While Charles was arranging to have his new "Sylph" bicycle made at a factory near Springfield, Frank worked there.

The two brothers were later to quarrel bitterly over which deserved more recognition for building their car, but it now seems clear that Charles thought of the idea and outlined it generally on paper in 1891. Frank then left his job and constructed the vehicle, working out most of the specific mechanical details as he went along.

The basis of the car was a second-hand carriage for ladies, bought by Charles for seventy dollars. The Duryeas then planned to add an engine, transmission and steering mechanism; but with Charles back in Peoria and giving advice by mail, Frank's progress was slow. For a time he was delayed by a bad case of typhoid fever, and he also ran into several serious mechanical problems.

Besides having to build a different type engine from that originally designed by Charles, Frank was forced to develop a new, electrical ignition system, devise a carburetor, and eventually invent a better

1893
Duryea

transmission for getting the engine's power to the wheels. Working until two A.M. morning after morning, he finally succeeded; and the car was able to travel about two hundred feet under its own power on September 21, 1893.

The one-cylinder, four-horsepower engine of

that first car was at its extreme rear, between the spindly forty-four-inch wheels. (The small tanks to be seen in the photograph above the engine are for gasoline and water.) Steering was done with a lever, called a tiller; and moving the tiller up and down also shifted gears.

An improved second Duryea, designed and built entirely by Frank, won the first automobile race to be held in the United States, fifty-five miles through snowy Chicago streets on Thanksgiving Day, 1895. Of six starters, only two finished; and the victorious Duryea averaged just over five miles an hour. The Duryea Motor Wagon Company had also been formed in 1895, and in 1896 it manufactured thirteen Duryeas for sale to the public. Charles and Frank were soon to disagree and pursue separate careers, but their short-lived company was the start of today's vast automotive industry.

Oldsmobile. Although some reports say the car was lost in a shipwreck, the first automobile to be exported from the United States was shipped to Bombay, India, in 1893. Built by Ransom Eli Olds of Lansing, Michigan, it was an improved version of a steam car that he had originally constructed six years earlier, when the Duryeas were still back in Peoria.

Olds was the son of a former blacksmith who

had given up shoeing horses for the more modern calling of operating a machine shop. Young Olds learned to be an expert machinist in his father's shop; and after he and his father had been making steam engines on a large scale for some time, they turned to the manufacture of gasoline engines.

Olds next attempted a gasoline-powered car, and, in common with other early automobile build-

1901
Oldsmobile

ers, found one of the biggest problems to be designing a workable gasoline engine that was small enough. Having completed the car in 1896, Olds then set up a company to make duplicates for sale; but he was much more successful than the Duryeas.

By 1901 the Olds Motor Works had developed no less than eleven different models, including some electric cars. That March, however, a raging fire swept through the factory, destroying everything. Everything that is except one small experimental runabout that a young worker was able to push out of the flames. The only survivor of the fire, it was immediately rushed into production.

Destined to become famous in a song — "Come Away With Me, Lucile, In My Merry Oldsmobile" — the light two-seater was much simpler and less expensive ($650) than the company's previous cars. With a wheelbase of only five and one-half feet and weighing but seven hundred pounds, the Merry Oldsmobile had a seven-horsepower, one-cylinder engine under its buggy-style seat. The thin wire-spoked wheels resembled those of a bicycle; the engine turned the rear axle by means of a chain; and there was no horn, a bicycle bell being standard equipment.

Steering was by tiller; and at its front the open carriage body swelled up into a graceful sleigh-like curve. For this reason this model is generally known as the curved-dash Oldsmobile. The photograph shows a 1901 car.

Ransom Olds was also a pioneer in automotive publicity; and tiny curved-dash Oldsmobiles were soon making demonstration climbs up the steps of many public buildings. They appeared at state fairs, too, where contests were often held to see how. many people could be crammed aboard, seventeen thin passengers seeming to have been the record.

The biggest curved-dash promotional stunt of them all was Roy Chapin's trip from Detroit to New York City in 1901. Roy Chapin was a young photographer with the Olds Motor Works who was asked by Ransom Olds to drive a Merry Oldsmobile all the way to New York for the Second National Automobile Show in Madison Square Garden. The 820-mile journey, partly through Canada, was the longest ever made by motor car at the time; and it took seven and one-half days of difficult travel over narrow, rutted and twisting roads. Since it was fall, at least there was no mud; and Chapin also saved time by running along the straight path that paralleled the Erie Canal, ordinarily used only by the mules that towed barges along the waterway.

In spite of bending the front axle in Canada, having to rebuild the transmission in Peekskill,

New York, and skidding into a Fifth Avenue curb, Chapin rolled up to the Waldorf Astoria Hotel right on schedule. He was so dirty from repairing a wheel after the skid, however, that the doorman would not let him in the front door and Chapin had to go around to the back.

This famous trip sent the sales of curved-dash Oldsmobiles quickly upward; and the small runabout became the most popular car of its day, the first to be sold in relatively large quantities. Surprisingly enough, within a few years the Olds management decided to stop making the Merry Oldsmobile, turning to larger and more powerful cars instead. Ransom E. Olds, who disagreed, left both the organization and automobile bearing his name behind in 1904; from then until 1936 he manufactured a car carrying his initials, the Reo.

Stanley. During the early days of the automobile in this country, there was strong rivalry among gasoline-, electric- and steam-propelled cars. Gasoline-powered vehicles eventually proved more practical, of course; but in the beginning many experts thought steam cars would win out.

The Stanley steam car was probably the best, and it was certainly the only steamer to have been built by identical twins, so similar in appearance that even their employees could not tell them apart.

F.E. and F.O. Stanley were former country school-teachers from Maine who had gone into business in Newton, Massachusetts, making photographic plates. At one time or another the bearded twins were also involved in the manufacture of violins, the invention of a home generator for lighting gas, and experimentation with early x-ray equipment.

1904
Stanley

Thus, when the versatile F.E. and F.O. saw a gasoline car from France break down during a demonstration run at the Brockton Fair, they decided to try building a car themselves. Their first "teakettle on wheels," finished in 1897, ran well; and after the twins had constructed two further-improved steamers, many people wanted to buy one. The Stanleys, always quick to know a good thing when they saw it, put their car into production in 1899.

When Stanley sales boomed, F.E. and F.O. showed themselves even shrewder businessmen by selling out for a quarter of a million dollars to individuals who ran things so poorly that the twins were soon able to buy their concern back for twenty thousand. They resumed making steamers in 1901 — a 1904 model is shown in the photograph — and continued until 1917 when both retired. The Stanley Motor Carriage Company then continued to produce cars, although at a steadily declining rate, until 1923.

Crusty individualists, the Stanleys sold only for cash, did not believe in advertising, and thought being asked to give a guarantee with one of their cars was an insult. As fast drivers themselves, they did regard racing as good publicity for a time, however. Special streamlined Stanleys, called "Wogglebugs," won many races; and Stanley cars were strong competitors during the annual winter "Speed Week" held on Ormond-Daytona Beach, Florida, in the early 1900's. Fred Marriott, head of the Stanley repair department, set a new World Land Speed Record of 127.66 mph there in 1906; but after his Bug crashed badly at 150 mph the following winter, the Stanleys gave up racing.

Stanley steamers were fast and smooth; very simple to drive and repair; and they were absolutely quiet. But Stanleys also required a long and complicated procedure of thirteen adjustments to get up steam before they could run; and many people unjustifiably feared a boiler explosion, too. In addition the handmade steam cars were much more expensive than mass-produced gasoline automobiles, so they gradually disappeared from the road.

Ford (Model T). Of all the five thousand makes and almost endless models of cars that have been built in this country and Canada, most important by far is the Model T Ford. Simple, tough and inexpensive, fifteen million Model T's were sold over a period of nineteen years; and they changed our way of life more than any other car.

In fact, Model T Fords became so well known all over the world that many people thought Henry Ford had invented the automobile. In reality his

1915
Ford Model T

first car, the "Quadricycle," was not completed until 1896, three years after the Duryea of 1893. Ford had made a rough sketch of the "Quadricycle" as early as 1891; but it was Christmas Eve, 1893, before he and his wife even tested his first gasoline engine in their kitchen sink.

Once the "Quadricycle" was running, Ford built two more experimental models and left his job as engineer for an electric lighting company to manufacture cars for sale. Not long afterward he also began building and driving racing cars for their publicity value; and at one point he held an unofficial World Land Speed Record of 91.37 mph.

Ford's first two attempts at manufacturing road cars were meanwhile both failures, but in 1903 his third try, the Ford Motor Company, was immediately successful. Among the original owners were the scrappy Dodge brothers, John and Horace, who gave up making transmissions for Oldsmobile to provide Ford with chassis, engines and transmissions built to Henry's designs. Except for bodies, wheels and a few other small parts, the Dodge brothers constructed all the Ford cars for the first three years, and a large proportion during the following seven. (In 1913 the Dodges were to leave Ford and start making their own automobiles. A much-told joke of the time claimed their cars needed no horns because they carried a warning on the front that read "Dodge Brothers.")

The first production Ford, a two-cylinder, Merry-Oldsmobile sort of car with its engine under the floor, was called Model A. In 1904 Model B, a much larger automobile with a four-cylinder engine, was also offered. Model C was an improved "A"; letters "D" and "E" were used for experimental models; and Model F, introduced in 1905, was a still-further-improved A. Sales of these cars were extremely good; and in 1906 the Ford Motor Company, then in only its fourth year, built more automobiles (8,729) than any other U.S. manufacturer.

A split had developed in its management, however, as reflected by Models K and N which came out late in 1905. Model K was a large and costly ($2,800) six-cylinder car, while Model N was a small, inexpensive ($500) four-cylinder vehicle; the argument was over whether to make luxury cars or automobiles for the average man. Henry Ford himself strongly favored the little N's, and when they sold much better than the big K's, the future course of the company was determined. R and S were built as fancy N's (1907), and next came the famous Model T.

The first Model T was made in 1908, the last in 1927; and during the intervening years millions of rattling, shaking flivvers poured out of the Ford factories to revolutionize daily living in the United States. For the first time a highly practical car was available that nearly everyone could afford, and as a result more and more Americans took to the road each year.

"Tin Lizzies" could run on any road in the

country, too, plus many places where there were no roads at all. The boxy Model T's were certainly no beauties; and with twenty-horsepower, four-cylinder engines they could only do forty miles an hour flat-out; but they were designed for rough use and were very sturdily built. In order to cover rough terrain their wheels were thirty inches in diameter and the springs were stiff; and Model T's were made of a special steel that was stronger and lighter than that used in other U.S. cars, even the most expensive. Called vanadium steel, it was first seen by Henry Ford when he examined the wreck of a French racing car on a Florida beach where he had brought a Model K to compete.

Besides being strong, T's were also very nimble, able to turn a circle in just a bit more than their length. They were also relatively easy to drive, the gears being shifted by means of foot pedals; and so simple to fix that an owner could do it himself. A farmer could even jack up his T, remove a rear wheel, belt his farm machinery to the rear axle and saw wood, grind grain or shear sheep.

With the price of a T getting down as low as $290 by 1924, there were no frills of any kind, not even a gas gauge; and the only way to tell how much gas was left was to stop, get out, unscrew the cap from the tank under the front seat, and put a stick inside. Since the gasoline was fed from the tank to the engine by gravity, it was often necessary to *back* up steep hills. And from 1914 until 1926, as Henry Ford himself said, you could have any color you liked, just as long as it was black. The reason was that black paint dried faster.

The T sold so well upon its introduction that the company quickly stopped making all the other model Fords to concentrate on increasing its production of T's. Even so, they could not be made fast enough to keep up with the great demand; and in 1913 Ford set up the first moving assembly line, reducing the time to build a car by more than one-half with this revolutionary manufacturing method. By 1915 there were over a million Model T's banging along U.S. roads, and from 1918 to 1925 they totaled more than one-half of all the cars in the country. The photograph is of a 1915 Model T.

3 / *Automobiles Become Big Business*

E.M.F. At the time Henry Ford decided to stop production of all other models and build only T's, not everyone thought he was making a wise move. One of those who disagreed was Walter E. Flanders, the Ford production manager who had developed the manufacturing procedures by which the Model T would be made.

Flanders left Ford in 1908, the year of the T's debut; and shortly afterwards he and two other automotive pioneers started the Everitt-Metzger-Flanders Company. B.F. Everitt was originally a carriage maker who had supplied upholstery for the curved-dash Oldsmobiles and who had also built the body for one of Henry Ford's first cars. "Smiling

Billy" Metzger was the former owner of a bicycle store who had become the first independent automobile dealer in the United States. In addition Metzger had been one of Henry Ford's early financial backers, a promoter of Detroit's first automobile race (won by Ford) and sales manager for Cadillac as well.

Although this trio also made a small twenty-horsepower "Flanders," their major car was the E.M.F. Thirty (photo), named for its horsepower. The E.M.F. had a wheelbase six inches longer than

E.M.F.

that of a Model T and cost $1,250. It was basically a sturdy enough automobile; but the gearbox was built as part of the rear axle, and this transmission-axle was subject to frequent failure. Consequently E.M.F. owners were always thinking up unflattering new names for their cars, ranging from "Every Man's Folly" to "Every Mechanical Fault"; with another favorite E.M.F. joke being to complain that the car needed service "Every Monday and Friday."

Everitt, Metzger and Flanders wanted an outside firm to handle the sales of their cars, for which they selected the Studebaker Brothers Manufacturing Company of South Bend, Indiana. The five Studebakers were then the country's largest builder of horse-drawn vehicles, but they had recently started to make horseless carriages, too; and the cars of both firms were to be sold together.

This arrangement was barely underway when Flanders and the Studebaker company got into divisive business and legal arguments. Studebaker finally settled the whole thing by buying up "Every Mechanic's Friend"; and while E.M.F. had a very brief existence from 1909 until 1913 Studebakers were made until 1966.

Buick. Brought to this country from Scotland in 1856 when he was two years old, David D. Buick was left an orphan at the age of five. He grew up in Detroit, and as a teen-ager his first mechanical job was with the same machine shop that was also to give Henry Ford his start a few years later.

Buick eventually became a partner in a plumbing-supply business; and he invented a process by which the porcelain coating is applied to cast-iron bathroom fixtures, thereby creating the first modern bathtub. At the turn of the century he sold his valuable plumbing interests to concentrate on building gasoline engines in which he had grown much more interested.

Buick's first engines were intended for use on farms and in boats, but before long he decided to build engines for those newfangled horseless carriages, too. The next logical step was to construct the automobiles themselves; and Buick's cars turned out to be stronger, more reliable and quieter than others of the early 1900's, primarily because of his superior engines. Buick and two of his engineers had located the valves in the head right over the pistons, and these "valve-in-head" engines were much more powerful for their size. (The same overhead-valve principle is still used today in nearly all automobile engines.)

As good as Buick's experimental model was, he was a much better inventor than businessman; and

1912
Buick

he had great difficulties getting his car into production. At first, Benjamin and Frank Briscoe, sheet-metal manufacturers known for their garbage cans and having supplied bodies to Ransom Olds, gave him materials and money in exchange for financial control of his company. Then, in 1903, the Briscoes decided this was a bad investment and sold out to a man from Flint, Michigan, who moved the company there.

The first twenty-seven production Buicks were

finally built in Flint during 1904, but by then the company was short of money again and had to be sold once more. This time control passed to a highly successful cart manufacturer and supersalesman, William C. Durant. He quickly made a great success of the organization at last; and by 1908 the Buick Motor Company was able to produce 8,820 cars, second only to Ford's 10,202.

Unlike Henry Ford who concentrated on one model at a time, Durant favored the modern practice of offering a wide variety of cars. In 1912, for instance, Buick buyers already had their choice of six models, including the sturdy touring car shown in the photograph.

Sad to say, David Buick had been squeezed out of the organization some time before. Tragically, the inventor Benjamin Briscoe once said had made a hundred other men millionaires was to have one business failure after another for the rest of his life and die in poverty. For that matter, hustling Billy Durant had also been toppled from power in Flint in 1910, but he was soon to regain leadership elsewhere in the rapidly expanding industry.

Maxwell. By July, 1894, less than a year after the Duryea made its first run in Massachusetts, a second successful internal combustion automobile had already been developed. Designed by Elwood

Haynes, a gas-company superintendent, the one-cylinder car was built in the Kokomo, Indiana, machine shop of the Apperson brothers.

One of the mechanics who worked on the car was Jonathan D. Maxwell, who later took a job at the Olds Motor Works where he became Chief Tester and worked on Roy Chapin's Detroit-to-New York car. Maxwell then left Olds to manufacture for a very short time a car that was at least partially of his own design, the "Silent Northern."

1911
Maxwell

During 1903 Maxwell also invented a system of engine cooling, the radiators for which were made by the Briscoe Manufacturing Company. Benjamin and Frank Briscoe had withdrawn their financial support from David Buick that same year; and when Maxwell designed a new car, Benjamin Briscoe went into partnership with him for its manufacture in Tarrytown, New York.

The first Maxwell-Briscoes, produced in 1904, were either a light two-passenger roadster with an eight-horsepower, two-cylinder engine that sold for $700; or a larger four-passenger touring car of fourteen horsepower costing $1550. As with several other early automobiles the handbrake of these Maxwells was connected to the clutch, so it was not necessary to use the clutch pedal when starting. Once the tiny engine was popping, easing off on the hand-brake alone would put the car in motion; and the clutch pedal was not needed until it was time to change gears.

The year after the Maxwell-Briscoe was introduced, Jonathan Maxwell drove a roadster and Benjamin Briscoe a touring car in the first Glidden Tour. Sponsored by Charles J. Glidden, a retired millionaire, the Glidden Tours were annual endurance runs held between 1905 and 1913 to demonstrate the reliability and convenience of the automobile as a new means of transportation. The demanding 870-mile route in 1905 started in New York City and wound through New England, including two difficult climbs of Mount Washington in New Hampshire.

A Pierce-Arrow won that first Glidden Tour; and Maxwell and Pierce, usually the lowest- and highest-priced cars on the tour, were to become bitter rivals throughout the remainder of the series. In 1911, the year of the Maxwell roadster in the photograph, a factory team of three Maxwells won the Glidden Trophy on a lengthy Tour from New York to Jacksonville, Florida.

The Maxwell company's best sales performance relatively speaking was in 1909 when it ranked right behind Ford and Buick. Jonathan Maxwell left in 1912 during a financial reorganization, with Walter Flanders coming in as head of the new management. (It had also been Flanders' E.M.F. group that had absorbed the company making Maxwell's "Silent Northern" in 1908.)

Faltering Maxwell fortunes made a second reorganization necessary in 1921; and former president of Buick Walter P. Chrysler was next to take over. Within a few years he was able to transform the company into the nucleus of today's powerful Chrysler Corporation, the little Maxwell first becoming a Chrysler and then being turned into the Plymouth in 1928.

Brush. Part of the time that his older brother Benjamin was involved with the Maxwell, Frank Briscoe was president of his own automobile manufacturing organization, the Brush Runabout Company. Named for its designer, Alanson P. Brush, the little Brush Runabout was even lower-priced ($485) than the Maxwell.

Brush had helped design the first Cadillac as well as the engine of the Oakland, a forerunner of the Pontiac; but he wanted the automobile named after him to be smaller and less costly. Like the curved-dash Oldsmobile and the Model T (Brush had gone to school with Henry Ford), the Brush Runabout was intended to be a simple and inexpensive car for the average family, costing less to buy and operate than a horse and buggy.

Only seven feet long and less than five feet wide, the Brush had a small one-cylinder, ten-horsepower engine that allowed the car a top speed of thirty miles an hour. The rear wheels were turned by chains, much like a bicycle, making Brushes good climbers; and a big lever located outside the body was used to shift gears.

While the Brush was thus quite similar to other cars of the period in many respects, it was markedly

1907
Brush

different in others. It was one of the first cars to have
a fuel pump instead of depending on gravity to get
gasoline into the engine, for instance. The Brush
was also one of the first cars in the United States to
have its driver located on the left side instead of on
the right side as was done in Europe, thus making it
easier for Americans to see ahead as they drove on
the right side of the road. And, in addition, the

Brush was one of the first automobiles in this country to have a coil-spring suspension.

Most unusual of all about the Brush, though, was the fact that it was made chiefly of wood for both lightness and low cost. Nearly all cars of that period had wooden wheels; but the body, frame and even the axles of the Brush were also wooden. The standard joke for the Brush owners was therefore that their car had a "wooden body, wooden axles, wooden wheels . . . and wooden run."

In spite of the joke, Brushes ran well enough as compared to other cars of the day; and in 1910 a little red Brush Runabout was used for a long test drive from New York City to Cross Roads, Oklahoma, by Bud and Temple Abernathy. Since Temple and Bud were ten and six years old at the time and had already ridden alone from Oklahoma to New York on horseback to meet their father, their trip was all the more incredible. Mr. Abernathy did not know how to drive, so he followed along behind the boys in a chauffeur-driven Maxwell.

Although advertised as "Everyman's Car," the Brush Runabout never really sold that well and was to have a brief life in the bargain. The first Brushes were made in 1907 (photo) and three years later the Brush organization became part of the ill-fated United States Motor Company. This was a large

General Motors-type combination of 130 companies headed by Benjamin Briscoe, with Maxwell-Briscoe as its base. Greatly overexpanded, the United States Motor Company went bankrupt in 1912, and only the Maxwell survived.

Briscoe. After the collapse of the United States Motor Company an undaunted Benjamin Briscoe went to France, where he set up Briscoe Frères to manufacture small cars. But by 1914 he had returned to this country to found the Briscoe Motor Company with money provided by the Swifts, a wealthy meat-packing family from Chicago.

Frank also had an interest in the Briscoe Motor Company, as had been true of most of Benjamin's other projects including financial help to Charles Duryea in 1907. This time the car, built in Jackson, Michigan, was named the "Briscoe"; and because Benjamin had brought its design back with him from France, he liked to call it "The First French Car at an American Price."

The Briscoe was a small car weighing only 1700 pounds, with a four-cylinder, twenty-four-horsepower engine in the first versions and a V-8 engine available in later years. The first models sold for $750, and in a signed advertisement Benjamin Briscoe explained that this price was very low because "we are satisfied with small profit" and "are not desirous of getting rich too rapidly." Possibly this was true, but the price was also low because it did not include the top, windshield, starter and generator, all of which were extras! An equipped Briscoe cost $900 initially, although it must be added that this price did come down in time and that other manufacturers also used similar pricing practices.

While not a particularly striking car in any other way, a Briscoe was instantly recognizable by its

1915
Briscoe

single headlight mounted at the top of the radiator. Bystanders never failed to take a second look when they spotted the "Cyclops Eye"; and as the photograph of a 1915 Briscoe touring car shows, many spectators at antique car meets still do so today.

Briscoe cars did not sell as well as those which the brothers had made under other people's names; and the Briscoe Motor Company had to stop production in 1922. Essentially the same automobile was then made as the Earl by another company for two more years.

Another irony of the Briscoe story is that Benjamin had brought plans for a very small motorcycle-type car back from France along with those for the bigger Briscoe; and he had also organized the Argo Motor Company in Jackson to manufacture this cyclecar. After only two years the unsuccessful Argo cyclecar became known as the Hackett; and three years later its manufacture was taken over by the Lorraine Motors Corporation of Grand Rapids. The Lorraine Motors Corporation existed for only two years before it, too, failed; and owning controlling interest at the time was David Buick.

4 / *The Automobile Age Arrives*

Chevrolet. Bushy-mustached Louis Chevrolet was one of three Swiss brothers, all racing drivers, who came to this country from France. In 1908 he and brother Arthur joined the factory racing team then being assembled by William Durant, who had recently taken control of Buick. The Buick racing team, formed by Durant to test engines as well as create publicity, won many races, traveling as far as Europe to compete.

Meanwhile, Durant was engaging in some competition of his own inside the executive offices. Using Buick as his base and later buying the Olds Motor Works, in 1908 he founded the General Motors Company which would eventually become the largest business enterprise in the world.

1918
Chevrolet

Durant's next move was to acquire more than twenty other companies for General Motors, including Cadillac and Oakland (now Pontiac), plus the rights to Frenchman Albert Champion's sparkplugs. Even Henry Ford hinted that he might sell to the aggressive Durant at this point; but the deal fell through when Ford specified that his eight-million-dollar price be paid in cash, something Durant was finding increasingly difficult to raise just then.

Part of Durant's trouble was caused by the many weak companies he had purchased; and successful as the Buick operation was, it could not make up for all these losses. By late 1910 General Motors had to borrow fifteen million dollars; and the lending bankers insisted that as one of the conditions for their loan Durant be removed from power.

Within a year Durant was back in action, however. In 1911 he formed the Mason Motor Company in Flint (Mason had formerly built Buick engines); the Little Motor Car Company in Flint (named after the ex-Buick general manager, not the size of its cars); and the Chevrolet Motor Company in Detroit. By then Louis Chevrolet had become a very famous racing driver; and in return for ownership of much of the company, he not only allowed the use of his name, he also designed — with some help — the first model of the Chevrolet.

A large, powerful and expensive six-cylinder automobile that cost $2,150, Chevrolet's design did not sell as well as the smaller $650 four-cylinder Littles. In 1913 Durant therefore combined the two companies for greater efficiency which so insulted Louis Chevrolet that he promptly left the organization and sold Durant all the stock that would have made him a very rich man. (Chevrolet was later to design the "American" automobile, a failure in spite of its cheery slogan, "America's Smile Car.")

The Chevrolet company then concentrated

more and more on building low-priced automobiles, the 490 Chevvie of 1915 being named after its eventual price. In 1917 Chevrolet built 110,839 cars; and as its production increased dramatically over the next ten years, it edged closer and closer to Ford for the national sales leadership. (A Chevrolet of 1918 is shown in the photograph.)

Finally, in 1927 when 1,749,998 Chevrolets were produced, Chevrolet became the best-selling car in the United States for the first time. The switch to a six-cylinder engine (nicknamed the "Cast Iron Wonder" and the "Stove-Bolt Six") was made in 1929; and from 1931 on Chevrolet has outsold all other U.S. cars in nearly every year.

This great advance by Chevrolet enabled William Durant to quietly trade Chevrolet stock for shares of General Motors; and by a 1915 GM Board of Directors' meeting he owned enough GM stock to walk in and announce that he controlled the company, completely flabbergasting the financial world. In 1916 Durant was therefore able to return as the central figure of General Motors for the second time.

Chevrolet was made a division of General Motors in 1918; and Durant stayed as overall head of the organization for the next two years. During the depression of 1920, however, he was again forced out of General Motors as part of still another major financial reorganization. Although he was to have a short period of success with Durant Motors after that, he was later reduced to declaring personal bankruptcy. Like David Buick, Durant died in obscurity.

Hudson. Three years after his historic drive from Detroit to the 1901 New York automobile show, Roy D. Chapin became the Olds Motor Works' first sales manager. Wanting to go into business for himself, he next left Olds in 1906 and got financial backing from E.R. Thomas. (Thomas automobiles were made in Buffalo, New York; and a Thomas Flyer was to win the astounding New York-to-Paris race of 1908, twenty-two thousand miles long and nearly around the world.)

Chapin was later joined by several other former Olds executives, including the man who had rescued the curved-dash Oldsmobile from the fire; and Howard Coffin, the very talented chief engineer at Olds. This group then formed a company to make automobiles designed by Coffin and sold to the public by Thomas.

In 1909, when Coffin had come up with a much-improved model, Chapin, Coffin and two other ex-Olds employees split off to set up still another organization. This time they received most of their money from J.L. Hudson, uncle of the wife of one member of the group and owner of Detroit's biggest department store; and the new car was called the Hudson. After all, as more than one writer has pointed out, they could hardly follow the usual custom of naming the car for its designer.

Hudsons quickly established themselves as solid, well-built cars; and over the years the Hudson Motor Car Company was responsible for several technical advances. One of these was an engine crankshaft that was weighted to be in perfect bal-

1923
Hudson

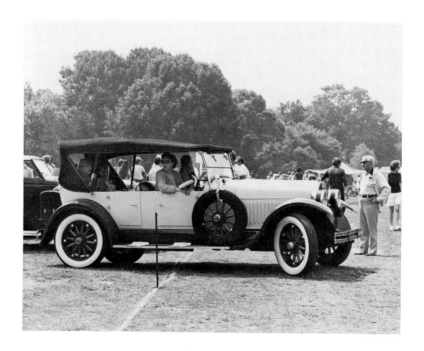

ance as it was spun around by the rods from the sliding pistons. First used in the 1916 Super-Six, this crankshaft not only smoothed out the usual violent engine shake of the time, it also permitted much higher crankshaft speeds, thereby producing more power from the same size engine.

The Hudson was first made as a low-priced four-cylinder car, then gradually became a medium-priced six-cylinder automobile of which the 1923 model in the photograph is an example. To broaden the line Chapin introduced the low-priced four-cylinder Essex (later called the Terraplane) in 1919; and the Essex soon became a strong rival of the Model T's.

Already more than twice as powerful as the T, the Essex gained another advantage in 1921. Until then the few totally enclosed "all-weather" cars were very expensive, the majority of automobiles having open bodies (photo) with folding cloth tops, and side curtains that could be buttoned on in case of cold or rain. As a result many people did not drive cars on bad days or in severe climates. By putting flat metal sheets over a box-shaped wooden frame, however, the builders of the Essex were able to give it a closed body costing only $300 more than the touring version.

After the Hudson had also received a similar

body, Chapin worked hard to bring the prices of his closed cars even lower; and by 1925 an Essex sedan cost only $895, which was five dollars *less* than an Essex tourer. This caused the other manufacturers to concentrate on building the more practical sedans too, a move that was to make automobiles sell even faster in the long run.

Chapin died in 1936, and by then the other "Olds alumni" had either died or retired, too. Only fifteen years remained for Hudson automobiles (no civilian cars were made for three years during World War II); and in 1954 the Hudson Motor Car Company had to be merged with another floundering automobile manufacturer, Nash, to form the present American Motors Corporation.

Cadillac. When Ransom Olds put the curved-dash Oldsmobile into production after the fire he needed engines in a hurry, so he placed orders with both the Dodge brothers and stern Henry M. Leland, who ran the best machine shop in Detroit. While each part of the Oldsmobile engine was required to measure within one one-hundredth of an inch of its specified size, this represented no problem at all to the demanding Leland because he was accustomed to allowing tolerances of only one-thousandth.

After Leland's shop had been turning out Oldsmobile engines for a time, his engineers made a special version that had several improvements and was built to one-thousandth-of-an-inch tolerances. This new engine was more than twice as powerful, but the Olds management decided to continue using the less precisely made original, probably for reasons of cost.

Shortly afterwards Leland was asked to appraise the machinery of the Henry Ford Company. This was the second of Henry Ford's two false starts before the success of the Ford Motor Company; Henry himself had just left and the company was about to go out of business. Instead of setting a value on the machinery, however, Leland recommended that the company stay in operation, using his Oldsmobile-type engine in its cars.

As a result the Henry Ford Company was reorganized in 1902 as the Cadillac Automobile Company, named for the French explorer who founded Detroit. The first Cadillacs, made in Leland's machine shop, were small, one-cylinder cars costing only $850; and they became very popular, outselling all other makes except Oldsmobile from 1904 until 1906. Nevertheless, Henry Leland and his son Wilfred had taken over management of Cadillac in 1904, and they were to gradually develop models of increasing quality and price.

Rather than continue making each part fit only one car as was generally done at the time, Henry Leland was one of the first to see the importance of building cars with standard interchangeable parts. As a demonstration of this idea in England in 1908, three Model K Cadillacs were taken apart, some parts changed for spares, all the parts scrambled and then assembled again. Each of the three cars ran perfectly for five hundred miles, and Cadillac was awarded the Dewar Trophy for the accomplishment.

A second Dewar Trophy was given Cadillac in 1913 for its electric self-starter and lighting system. Cadillac's starter was the first practical device of its kind, finally ending the nuisance and danger of hand-cranking cars to start them. Since the Cadillac needed a large battery to supply power for its starter anyway, the Lelands' engineers took advantage of it to also provide the car with electric lights. These two advances, soon adopted by other car makers as well, added greatly to the general use of automobiles.

Henry and Wilfred Leland left Cadillac in 1917 to later build another luxury car, named after Henry's idol, Abraham Lincoln. By then Cadillac had been owned by William Durant's General Motors for eight years; and as part of that giant cor-

1924
Cadillac

poration it has continued making prestigious vehicles until the present. The photograph shows a 1924 model.

Packard.   The first of two traditional Packard stories is an explanation of why James W. Packard built his own automobile in the first place. This anecdote relates that in 1898 Packard bought Alexander Winton's twelfth car (Wintons were made in Cleveland, Ohio, from 1897 until 1924), that the car broke down time after time, and that Packard complained angrily to Winton. An insulted Winton is then supposed to have snapped something like "If you think you can do better, try it," whereupon

Packard is said to have replied, with much determination, "I will!"

In reality it is likely that James Packard and his brother William had already been thinking about building a car long before this happened. Whatever the circumstances, they did hire two men away from Winton and started constructing an automobile in a corner of the Warren, Ohio, factory where they made electrical supplies. The Model A Packard, a one-cylinder runabout first called an "Ohio," was completed in 1899; and it was such a good automobile that James Packard decided to put it on the market.

According to the second favorite Packard story, it was about this time that the famous slogan originated. A letter is reported to have arrived at the factory asking for a sales pamphlet describing the car; and because none was yet available, James Packard is quoted as instructing, "Tell them to . . . 'Ask the Man Who Owns One.'"

By 1901 the Model C Packard already had a steering wheel in place of a tiller, the first car to do so. The 1901 Packard was the first automobile to have its gearshift lever move in the now-familiar "H" pattern, too. But unfortunately for James Packard, 1901 was also the year in which he began to lose control of the company he had started.

Henry B. Joy, the son of a founder of the Chicago, Burlington and Quincy Railroad, had gone to the New York automobile show that fall to buy a car. (This was the same show to which Roy Chapin had driven the Oldsmobile.) Joy quickly decided against a steamer that was displayed there after it had showered him with hot water; but when he saw a man start a Model C Packard at the curb with a single twirl of the crank to chase a horse-driven fire engine, he bought one like it.

Back home and well satisfied with his Packard, Joy invested heavily in the company and soon came to dominate its management. He moved the Packard organization to Detroit in 1903, eventually taking over as president from James Packard, who chose to remain in Warren.

The first car to be driven across the United States was a secondhand two-cylinder, twenty-horsepower Winton owned by a doctor from Vermont. To collect a fifty-dollar bet, he left San Francisco in late May, 1903, and arrived in New York City sixty-four days later. The second automobile to complete the adventurous four-thousand-mile journey was a much smaller one-cylinder, twelve-horsepower Model F Packard called "Old Pacific." Driven by a Packard shop foreman and an early automotive writer, "Old Pacific" left San Francisco four weeks after "The Vermont" and beat the larger Winton's record by three days.

In 1915 the public was so astonished by the new Twin-six Packard, which had a twelve-cylinder, eighty-five horsepower engine with the first aluminum pistons, that showrooms had to stay open all night. Later a racing car was built with a modified version of this engine; and in 1919 on Ormond-Daytona Beach it set a new U.S. Land Speed Record of 149.875 mph.

Like Cadillac, the Packard company became prosperous during the Twenties and early Thirties

1931
Packard

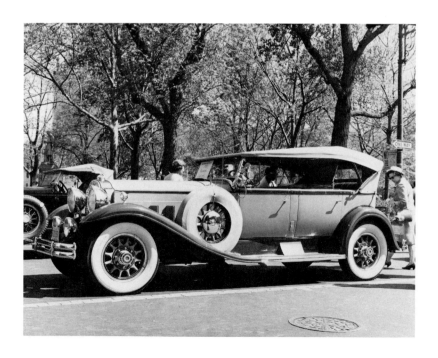

by building long, luxurious and expensive cars. (The eight-cylinder 1931 model in the photograph has a second windshield to protect passengers in the rear seat when the top is down.) But both the quality and sales of Packards declined sharply after World War II, and the once-great make slowly collapsed during the mid-Fifties.

Ford (Model A). By 1927 even Henry Ford himself had to agree that his elderly Model T was out of date. Other low-priced cars had become more powerful and were more comfortable, included such recent improvements as self-starters in their standard equipment, and also came in more colors. Sales of T's were falling off badly, which meant that a new model was needed as soon as possible.

Unlike today, when a new model is developed at the same time an old one is still being made, the Ford factory simply shut down in late May of 1927 and did not start production again until that October. An entirely new Ford was designed, its prodection methods worked out, and the machinery needed to make the car devised during that relatively short interval.

All this was done in the deepest secrecy as curiosity steadily increased throughout the United States. Some said the new Ford would have six cylinders, some thought it would be a V-8, and still others were absolutely certain that it would be named"Edison" after the inventor who was a close friend of Henry Ford's. Without even knowing its price, 500,000 people placed deposits on the car, whatever it turned out to be; and as a news story that year the coming of the new Ford ranked second only to Lindbergh's trans-Atlantic flight.

With suspense heightening all the more, the much-awaited new models finally began to arrive at dealers' showrooms covered with canvas so they still could not be seen. Then, when they were displayed at last, the milling crowds grew so large in several cities that police had to be called in to restore order.

What the excited viewers saw were cars like the snappy little roadster in the photograph. Except for having the same springs, the same number of cylinders (four) and a similar low starting price ($385), they were nothing at all like the Model T. Perhaps to show just how new they were, the Ford company had gone all the way back to the beginning of the alphabet again and called them "Model A."

The Model A was almost a foot lower and two feet longer than a Model T with much more up-to-date styling. Its forty-horsepower engine gave the A a top speed of sixty miles an hour, and for the first time a Ford had four-wheel brakes. There was a standard three-speed transmission that was shifted by hand instead of with foot pedals like the T; and the A's accelerator was worked by foot instead of by hand. The Model A Ford was also the first low-priced car to have a safety-glass windshield; and just in front of the windshield was the cap of the gas-tank by which any Model A can be easily spotted.

Nearly five million A's of only slightly differing specifications were made during the model's four-year history; but in 1932 the Model A had to be dropped in favor of still newer V-8 models to keep

Ford Model A

up with the fast-selling Chevrolet sixes. The end of the Model A thus marked the beginning of the modern automobile age; from then on an annual model change, even if only a slight change of appearance, became common as competition intensified. The fifty-millionth U.S. motor vehicle had already been made the year before; and if that was not enough of a signal that the automobile was revolutionizing American life, the year after the Model A was withdrawn from production, the first drive-in movie in the country opened.

5 / *Seeing Antique Cars*

A GOOD WAY TO GET A close-up look at cars like those in the preceding chapters is to visit a museum. The "first," very-oldest or only-known specimens are apt to be found in the transportation sections of large general museums or local historical collections. For instance, the Smithsonian Institution of Washington, D.C., exhibits the 1893 Duryea, the 1894 Haynes, the last remaining Olds of 1897 and the 1903 coast-to-coast Winton.

As you might expect, the Henry Ford Museum in Dearborn, Michigan, has many early Fords, including the 1896 "Quadricycle"; but a large number of other makes, such as an 1896 Duryea and the "Old Pacific" Packard, can also be seen there. And, as one further example, the Sloan Museum of Flint,

Michigan, contains William Durant's first cart, a 1910 Buick from his racing team and the very first Chevrolet.

In addition to these, there is also a much larger group of specialized museums devoted exclusively to old cars. While these museums may have a small number of very early or rare vehicles on display, too, their basic objective is to show representative examples of the many production automobiles of the past. Most inclusive by far is Harrah's Automobile Collection in Reno, Nevada, which now

"Get close, but please don't touch!"

totals more than 1,400 cars; but there are may other excellent collections in all parts of the coutry. A list of some of the major automotive collections and museums in the United States and Canada is the final chapter of this book.

In many respects, attending an antique car show can be even more fun. They are ordinarily held out of doors, are often accompanied by old-time music, and usually have snack tents like a carnival. At an outdoor meet spectators not only see a wide variety of vehicles at rest, they can watch — and hear — them in motion. There can also be opportunities to talk with the owners of the cars and ask them questions; once in a while there may even be a chance to ride in an antique car.

(While it is possible to get close enough to the cars at an outdoor meet to touch them, please don't. Rare to begin with, antique cars have been painstakingly rebuilt and are therefore of great value. Then, too, the owner is likely to have been up very late the night before the show polishing all that brass; he won't like fingerprints, even admiring ones.)

At most meets the cars are judged for the accuracy of their restoration within categories, prizes being awarded at the end of the day. The detailed examination of the judges as they hover over and

An antique automobile horn goes up for auction.

under each car interests many spectators; and a crowd also collect when the performance tests are held. These include such events as attempts to balance a car at the center of a giant seesaw in the fastest time, races to see who can get his or her crank-type car started first, and speed competitions among the owners of touring cars at putting up their complicated tops.

Another typical feature of most antique car

meets is the flea market where old automobile parts are swapped and sold. The hobby of restoring old cars has now become so popular that some replacement parts are being made again; but the original items are usually preferred, despite surface rust and grease. They can be quite hard to find, of course; so flea-market searchers can occasionally be seen with "Wanted" signs on their backs or in their hats listing parts they currently need but have not been able to locate.

Unless you know someone who has an antique car, or wait until you see several well-shined beauties spinning along the highway early on a weekend morning and follow them, it may be difficult to learn just when an antique car show is to be held in your area. Public libraries should be able to help here, particularly if they subscribe to either "Old Cars" or "Hemmings Motor News."

These publications also list when and where the less-common antique car auctions take place. You might like to attend one of these, too, and see how some enthusiasts buy and sell both parts and entire cars. If a 1929 Model J Duesenberg comes on the block while you are there, don't nod at the auctioneer, though. The last one to be sold brought two hundred and seven thousand dollars.

6 / *Antique Car Museums*

ARKANSAS	The Museum of Automobiles	Route 3, Morrilton
CALIFORNIA	Briggs Cunningham Automotive Museum	250 E. Baker St., Costa Mesa
	Los Angeles County Museum of Natural History	900 Exposition Boulevard, Los Angeles
	Movieworld Cars of the Stars	6920 Orangethorpe Ave., Buena Park
COLORADO	Forney Transportation Museum	1416 Platte Street, Denver
DISTRICT OF COLUMBIA	Smithsonian Institution, Museum of History and Technology, Vehicle Hall	Constitution Ave. at 14th St.
FLORIDA	Bellm Cars of Yesterday	5500 North Tamiami Trail, Sarasota
	Early American Museum	Route 40, Silver Springs
	Elliott Museum of Vehicular Evolution	Route 5, Stuart
GEORGIA	Antique Auto and Music Museum	2542 Young Road, Stone Mountain
ILLINOIS	Chicago Historical Antique Automobile Museum	3160 Skokie Valley Road, Highland Park
	Museum of Science and Industry	Jackson Park, Chicago

KANSAS	Billue's Antique Car Museum	Route 81, Hesston
MASSACHUSETTS	Heritage Plantation of Sandwich	Grove and Pine Sts., Sandwich
	Museum of Transportation	15 Newton St., Brookline
	Sturbridge Auto Museum	Route 20, Sturbridge
MICHIGAN	Detroit Historical Museum	5401 Woodward Ave., Detroit
	Greenfield Village and Henry Ford Museum	Oakwood Blvd., Dearborn
	Poll Museum	353 East 6th St., Holland
	Sloan Museum	303 Walnut St., Flint
MINNESOTA	Hemp Museum	Country Club Road, Rochester
MISSOURI	Autos of Yesteryear	Route 63, Rolla
	Kelsey's Antique Cars	Route 564, Camdenton
NEBRASKA	Harold Warp Pioneer Village	Routes 6 and 34, Minden
NEVADA	Harrah's Automobile Collection	East 2nd St., Reno
NEW JERSEY	Roaring 20 Autos	Route 34 and Ridgewood Rd., Wall
NEW YORK	Long Island Automotive Museum	Route 27, Southhampton
	Upstate Auto Museum	Route 20, Bridgewater
OHIO	Crawford Auto-Aviation Museum	10825 East Blvd., Cleveland
OKLAHOMA	Horseless Carriages Unlimited	2215 West Shawnee St., Muskogee
PENNSYLVANIA	Automobilorama	Route 15, Harrisburg
	Boyertown Museum of Historic Vehicles	Warwick St., Boyertown
	Pollock Auto Showcase	Route 30, Downingtown
	Swigart Museum	Route 22, Huntingdon
SOUTH DAKOTA	Horseless Carriage Museum	Route 16, Rapid City
VIRGINIA	Roaring Twenties Antique Car Museum	Route 230, Hood
ALBERTA, CANADA	Reynolds Museum	Highway 2A, Wetaskiwin
SASKATCHEWAN, CANADA	Western Development Museum	2610 Lorne Ave. S., Saskatoon